Berthe Morisot

PLATE I

Berthe Morisot

DRAWINGS / PASTELS / WATERCOLORS

INTRODUCTION by ELIZABETH MONGAN
Curator of Prints and Drawings, National Gallery of Art, Washington, D. C.

PREFACE by DENIS ROUART
Conservateur du Musée des Beaux-Arts de Nancy

RESEARCH and CHRONOLOGY by ELAINE JOHNSON
Department of Prints and Drawings, Museum of Modern Art, New York

CATALOG COMMENTARY by REGINA SHOOLMAN

GENERAL EDITOR: IRA MOSKOWITZ

Published by Shorewood Publishing Co., Inc., New York
in collaboration with
Charles E. Slatkin Galleries, New York

Cover and Book Design: Fred Hausman

Library of Congress Catalog Card Number: 60-53214

PRINTED IN THE U.S.A.

To

Julie Manet Rouart

TABLE OF CONTENTS

PLATE II

Berthe Morisot

An Exhibition of Drawings

DRAWINGS / PASTELS / WATERCOLORS

at the

MUSEUM OF FINE ARTS, Boston, Mass.
October 10th to November 8th, 1960

CHARLES E. SLATKIN GALLERIES, New York
November 12th to December 10th, 1960

CALIFORNIA PALACE OF THE LEGION OF HONOR
December 20th to January 18th, 1961 San Francisco, Calif.

MINNEAPOLIS INSTITUTE OF FINE ARTS
January 25th to February 23rd, 1961 Minneapolis, Minn.

PLATE III

Watercolor, 6½ x 10 inch, Collection of John S. Newberry.

Berthe Morisot

1841-1895

by ELIZABETH MONGAN

Berthe Morisot was an artist *de race.* Everyone who ever knew her or wrote about her work eventually turns to the descriptive adjective "charming." As artist, as a friend, as a woman she was exactly that. It would be a misinterpretation, however, to accept the term in its present American connotation, as meaning a kind of superficial pleasantness and carefully groomed appearance. Berthe Morisot's charm was entirely French of her epoch in quality and character. It was based on personal distinction, wit, cultivated intelligence, femininity and grace. It was also the product of a strict education in a definite milieu.

Berthe Morisot, the third daughter of four children, was born in Bourges in 1841. Her father, Edme-Tiburce Morisot, had originally prepared at the Ecole des Beaux-Arts for a career in architecture. In his choice of a profession he was following in the footsteps of his father, Josephin Morisot, a successful architect and the author of a voluminous book on the practice of architecture. Tiburce Morisot after traveling widely in Italy, Sicily and Greece, instead of entering upon a career in architecture, settled into government service. When Berthe was born, he was prefect, or the chief administrative official, in the Department of Cher. Seven years later, after being prefect in a number of provincial towns, Tiburce Morisot was transferred to Paris. There he remained almost continuously in official positions, as an able administrator and counsellor, until his death in 1874. It is interesting to add that it was on her father's side that Berthe Morisot was the great-niece of Fragonard.

Her mother, Marie Corneille Thomas, had married at sixteen. The men in the Thomas family were generally treasurers and paymasters. Through the influence of her beloved mother, Berthe perceived the necessity for developing and guarding all the outward feminine gestures of her period, but she seems to have inherited as well her keen, analytical, rather masculine mind. When the time came, she could appraise the work of even her very close friends with remarkable objectivity.

The young Berthe and her two elder sisters Yves and Edma, with whom she retained the closest and most affectionate bonds all her life, were brought up together in a sympathetic, comfortable Parisian household. (Yves later married Paul Gobillard, and her daughter, Jeanne, in 1900 married Paul Valéry.) Both Edma and Berthe began to draw when they were very young. Their immature talent was regarded with pleasure by both their parents. When Berthe was sixteen, it was arranged that the two girls should take their first formal lessons from an obscure master named Geoffroy-Alphonse Chocarne, who lived in the Rue de Lille. His mediocre instruction did not last long. After several months both Edma and Berthe complained to their mother that they would rather give up all idea of painting rather than spend four hours three times a week with Chocarne. They were precocious in their judgment and already serious in their intentions. Their next teacher, circa 1858, was Guichard, a painter originally from Lyons. He had worked in the studio of Ingres, but subsequently had been attracted by the theories of Delacroix. Under his tutelage, the two gifted young women received a sound training in draughtsmanship. They also absorbed a sense of the continuity of tradition in great French art. According to Tiburce Morisot, the younger brother of Berthe, Guichard after he had seen one of the sketches made by Berthe during her first lesson, took Madame Morisot aside and in a rather nervous way said, "Your daughters have such inclinations that my teaching will not give them the small talent of pleasing; they will become painters. Do you realize what that means? In your environment of the upper-middle class this will be a revolution, I might almost say a catastrophe. Are you quite sure that you will never curse the day that art, entering your respectable, peaceful house will become the only master of the destiny of your two children?" When Madame Morisot smiled and agreed to continue with Guichard, the latter replied, "Then, the first thing to do is to ask for an authorization for permission to work in the Louvre where I will give them lessons before the masters." The Morisot girls began to copy the old masters in the Louvre in the spring of 1858. There they met two other young artists, Bracquemond, formerly a pupil of Guichard, and Fantin-Latour. Berthe, at that time, was especially susceptible to the Venetian painters of the sixteenth century. She loved the splendor and the color that she found in their pictures. She made, in turn, very creditable copies of *The Crucifixion* and the *Feast in the House of Simon* by Paul Veronese. Little by little she was gaining her objective. Up until then she had always worked indoors, in a studio or in the Louvre. Now she began to want to paint out of doors, although all her life she returned to the Louvre from time to time to study. Even when a mature and recognized artist, she set herself the task of copying Mantegna and Boucher. Guichard, who had no real feeling for nature, but was honest, resigned himself to the inevitable. He took his accomplished pupil to Corot.

In 1861 the Morisot family passed the summer at Ville d'Avray, where Corot lived and painted. The influence of the genial landscape painter, then past sixty, was very important for the two young ladies. With exceptional generosity Corot shared with them his vision of light and his understanding of form. It was the beginning of a very satisfying friendship. Not only did Corot instruct them, but he soon adopted the custom of dining every Monday night at their parents' house, with the understanding that he might smoke his pipe after dinner. In 1863 when Corot planned to be away on a trip, he thoughtfully and characteristically proposed that his two young friends should continue their work with his pupil, Oudinot. The good Oudinot, in turn, introduced them to Daubigny and, what for their development was more significant, to the mellow Daumier, then at the height of his power as a draughtsman. Berthe and Edma spent the summer painting out of doors on the river Oise between Pontoise and Auvers. By steps that seemed almost natural but really through family friendships and connections, they had been guided and given an exceptional education in painting and drawing, especially when one considers that they were young French ladies. The name of Aimé Millet, the sculptor, should be added to the list of Berthe's teachers. For a short time Berthe took lessons from him in modeling, lessons she never forgot. It was in Millet's studio that she made an intimate and life-long friendship with the Duchess of Colonna, who used the pseudonym Marcello to sign her sculpture.

Gradually both Edma and Berthe began to extend their visual experience by travel. In 1862 they had made a trip to the Pyrenees. But, it was through their visits to various regions in the French countryside that their acute perception of light and color became the real subject matter of their compositions. In 1869 Edma married Adolphe Pontillon, a naval officer and devoted her life and energies to him and her family. Berthe was at Beuzeval, in Normandy in 1864. Two of her paintings done that summer were sent to and accepted by the Salon. Her career as an artist in her own right had begun.

It has been said by one of Berthe Morisot's biographers that she wrote very little and that her life was singularly undisturbed and calm. While it is true that her fugitive sketches and numerous water-colors were often intended as a kind of day-by-day record, an artist's diary, it is also a fact that she wrote continuously to her family and friends all her life. Her letters are full of information about herself and the progress of her work. They also contain discriminating criticism not only of her friends' work but of the art of the period as well. There is little gossip and no malice, a rare thing in her artistic world where feuds were often acrimonious and cruel. Her letters also make it clear that she suffered intensely, even to the point of physical illness, when she felt that her work went badly, when friends or relations died, and when the disaster of the German occupation of Paris took place. As one would expect, she had a very sensitive and precise command of the French language.

PLATE IV

Berthe and Edma continued to send their paintings to the Salon for the next few years. They were mainly scenes painted in Normandy and Brittany. At the same time Berthe persevered with her studies in the Louvre. It was there, while she was copying a detail from the Marie de Medici series by Rubens, that she met Edouard Manet. Their admiration for each other was immediate. He was attracted by the mobility of her face, her deep-set, pensive eyes and her distinction of figure and dress. He had previously seen and liked her paintings in the Salon. She was drawn to the man through his sincerity and his volatile spirits and to his work because of the virtuosity of his brush-work. The deep and lasting friendship which followed was certainly to the advantage of both. Her painting became freer in technique and more daring. He came to a better realization of the subtle challenge of painting *en plein air*. Until then Manet had painted almost entirely indoors. The real ambition of both was the same, to place fully realized, casual human beings in the vibrant atmosphere of nature.

Inevitably Berthe Morisot became a member of the Impressionist circle. She no longer sent her work to the Salons but contributed instead to the impressionist exhibitions. In December 1874, in the church at Passy, Berthe Morisot married Eugène Manet, the brother of the painter. Her only daughter, Julie Manet, was born in 1878.

All of the drawings, pastels and water-colors included in the present exhibition date from the years after her marriage until her death (1880-1894). The models were chosen from her own small world. They represent her daughter Julie, pictured from infancy through adolescence, and her favorite niece, Jeannie Gobillard, as she also passed from her cradle to young womanhood. In the winter Berthe Morisot used as a subject for a sketch (Pl. 47) the daughter of her concierge in her house in the Rue Villejust. In summer a young peasant seen in the village as Mézy carrying a milk jug (Pl. 2) served as the first idea for a painting of the same subject. There are a few enchanting sketches of children at play in parks, water-colors of fishermen, birds swimming through water and delicate studies of flowers and trees. When in Paris the artist went from her studio, painted white with rose curtains, through her tiny city garden to the Bois-de-Boulogne and back. She carried pencils, colored crayons and paper continuously. Whenever she was staying at Mézy or at Cimiez, the same rule was followed. Her method of work was usually to start with a light pencil sketch, to repeat or vary the theme in sanguine, to remodel the composition in pastel and, quite often, to carry forward the theme in water-color and occasionally to carry it to a final culmination in a finished oil.

The two infants, Julie Manet (Child in Bed, Pl. 18, pastel) and Jeannie Gobillard in white (Pl. 51, pastel), are drawn with an easy surety. The solid form of the chubby, engaging infants is created through a few significant charcoal accents, not through contours. These accents are supplemented by white chalk, which suggests clothing. One feels the warmth of the maternal eye. A little later (Pl. 29) the two young cousins are pictured *vis à vis* seemingly in conversation. Here the juxtaposition of colors helps to heighten the sense of spontaneity and the freshness of childhood. The two little girls in deep blue dresses, seated in pale yellow chairs, are placed against a background of blue paper on which the addition of a few pink lines give a needed touch of light, creating the illusion of atmosphere. In the beautiful sanguine head of Julie (Pl. 5) and the two heads of Julie and Jeanne Gobillard (Pl. 61) the inner spirituality of each is felt and brought out delicately, animating the drawing with an unmistakable poignancy that is Berthe Morisot's personal contribution. It is a rare and exceptional gift in an artist to be able to produce such an interpretation of youth without slipping into banality or sentimentality.

Berthe Morisot's long, extraordinary friendship with the poet Mallarmé was partly based on their mutual, intense dislike of anything vulgar in art or life. There was also her instinctive perception of and sympathy with the symbolist ideas as they were spoken or written by the poet. In a letter that she wrote home from Italy in 1881 she said, "on s'agite, on se tremousse, on ne comprend plus que rien ne vaut deux heures étendues sur une chaise-longue—le rêve c'est la vie et le rêve est plus vrai que la realité; on y agit soi, vraiment soi. Si on a une âme elle est là."*

The graceful swans (pastel, Pl. 40) could have easily served as an illustration for a poem by Mallarmé. She loved to draw the birds on the quiet pond in the Bois-de-Boulogne especially in the pale grey hours near dawn or late in the day when a mauve twilight pervades the park. The swan becomes a symbol. Through a few touches of colors, green, pink and yellow on blue paper she was able to suggest the slight tremor of apprehension, an uneasy melancholy that passes almost unconsciously to the senses.

The moving self-portrait, (pastel, Pl. 1) was done later in her life. It is deeply poignant and unforgettably revealing, especially if juxtaposed with a letter written to her daughter and niece on the eve of her death.

"Ma petite Julie, je t'aime mourante; je t'aimerai encore morte; je t'en prie, ne pleure pas; cette séparation était inévitable; j'aurais voulu aller jusqu'à ton mariage . . . Travaille et sois bonne comme tu l'as toujours été; tu ne m'as pas causé un chagrin dans ta petite vie. Tu as la beauté, la fortune; fais-en bon usage. Je crois que le mieux serait de vivre avec tes cousines, rue de Villejust, mais je ne t'impose rien. Tu donneras un souvenir de moi à ta tante Edma et à tes cousines; à ton cousin Gabriel, les *Bateaux en reparation,* de Monet. Tu diras à M. Degas que s'il fonde un musée, il choisisse un Manet. Un souvenir à Monet, à Renoir et un dessin de moi à Bartholomé.

* One dashes about and fusses; one no longer realizes that nothing is more important than a couple of hours stretched out on a hammock; life is a dream and the dream is more true than reality—there one is oneself, really oneself. If one does have a soul, that is where it is to be found.

Tu donneras aux deux concierges. Ne pleure pas; je t'aime encore plus que je t'embrasse. Jeannie, je te recommande Julie."*

The fibre of the woman and artist is in both these last testaments.

* "My little Julie, I love you as I die; I shall still love you even when I am dead; I beg you not to cry, this parting was inevitable. I hoped to live until you were married . . . Work and be good as you have always been; you have not caused me one sorrow in your little life. You have beauty, money; make good use of them. I think it would be best for you to live with your cousins, Rue de Villejust, but I do not wish to force you to do anything. Please give a remembrance from me to your aunt Edma and to your cousins; and to your cousin Gabriel give Monet's *Bateaux en réparation*. Tell M. Degas that if he founds a museum he should select a Manet. A souvenir to Monet, to Renoir, and one of my drawings to Bartholome. Give something to the two concierges. Do not cry; I love you more than I can tell you. Jeannie, take care of Julie."

PLATE V

Baltimore Museum of Art (Cone Collection).

Collection of the California Palace of the Legion of Honor, San Francisco.

PLATE VI

PLATE 37

PORTRAIT STUDIES OF JEANNE PONTILLON [1893]

Watercolor, 11¼ x 8½ in. (29 x 22 cm) ; atelier stamp lower left.

Bibliography: p. Angoulvent no. 522; Bataille no. 799; Correspondence (reprod. opp. page 170).

Exhibited: p. Durand-Ruel 1896 no. 301.

The water color sketched in preparation for the portrait of Jeanne Pontillon (B. 338) shows the young girl in two poses: at left, her body follows the curving line of the sofa, at the right she is shown in profile, her arms folded, nestling more solidly into the curve of the sofa back. The eye moves from pose to pose, noting the shifting of the model's position, as the artist herself must have shifted her own chair and studied the possibilities of each angle.

Berthe Morisot

PLATE 1

SELF-PORTRAIT [1885]

Pastel, 18 x 14 in. (46 x 36 cm.) ; atelier stamp lower right.

Bibliography. Bataille no. 479.

Theodore Duret says that Berthe Morisot was not really beautiful, that her features lacked regularity and her complexion was not brilliant. Yet it was impossible, he says, not to notice her, for she was an artist to her fingertips. "She was graceful, very distinguished, and perfectly natural. The slender, nervous body betrayed the sensitive impressionable temperament . . . whatever she did came straight from the heart and was full of charm and sensitivity of spirit. There was a perfect accord between her and her work." These are the qualities that drew the Manets to her, and that won the devotion of Renoir, Degas and the poet Mallarmé. Here is a portrait in the great tradition, the eyes a bit sunken, staring through the shimmer of the mirror, the mouth terse, for she did not suffer fools gladly, the nose thin, the chin strong, the look self-appraising. For she has been uncompromising with herself, while her art has been a mission of high seriousness which never gives her rest. One sees the evidences of struggle, the note of melancholy highlighted in these quick slashes of accent. Here is dazzling virtuosity of the pastel which even Manet could have envied.

Berthe Morisot

PLATE 4

EUGENE AND JULIE MANET; INTERIOR; ISLE OF JERSEY [1886]

Pastel, 18 x 23½ in. (46 x 60 cm.) ; Bataille 511, Angoulvent 278.

In much that Berthe Morisot wrote and painted, one senses the reticence of a fastidious mind; reticence was the keynote to her husband's character as well. In her *oeuvre* he remains a rather shadowy figure, for, as she confided to her sister, "He is not an obliging model; at once it becomes too much for him."

The interior of the country house on the Isle of Jersey, with its bay window overlooking the sea, affords one of the rare glimpses into the life of the family of which Eugène Manet was the head. He is half hidden behind the newspaper which absorbs his attention, while little Julie gazes out of the window at the boats gliding by. The room is flooded with sun; a breeze moves the fluttering curtains, but the atmosphere is quiet and muted in keeping with the figure reading behind the table. One has no definite impression of him as a personality; for that, one must turn to the very human portrayal by his friend, Edgar Degas, done in the summer of 1874, the year of his marriage to Berthe.

If Eugène Manet was romantic, talented, gifted with imagination and *esprit*, none knew it but his intimates, for he shunned the limelight. And so his wife portrayed him in this sunlit room, quiet and withdrawn, yet inescapably part of her life—the man of whom she wrote, after his death: "I have descended to the depths of suffering, and it seems to me that after that one cannot help being raised up. But I have spent the last three nights weeping."

This pastel was used as a study for the oil, *Interior, Isle of Jersey* (A. 282), now in the *Musée d'Ixelles*, Belgium.

PLATE 11

STUDY OF THE GARDEN AT RUE DE VILLEJUST [1883]

Pastel, 15¾ x 20½ in. (40 x 52 cm.); atelier stamp lower right.
Bibliography: Bataille no. 472

Only slowly and hesitantly did recognition come to Berthe, at first from her own colleagues: "Manet came to see us Tuesday evening and we all went into the studio. To my great surprise and satisfaction, I received the highest praise." Mary Cassatt came to admire and stayed for friendship. Word of Berthe's brilliant brushwork gradually got around. Her devoted admirers, Manet, Renois, Degas, urged her to continue to exhibit with them. Finally, by the Seventh Impressionist Exhibition of 1882 the group had won a grudging acceptance. A letter arrives for Berthe: "Edouard Manet who came to the exhibition this morning says that your pictures are among the best . . ."

The following year Berthe moved into the newly built house on the Rue de Villejust where she spent many happy hours with her husband and daughter. From her studio window overlooking the garden, she sketched her daughter and a playmate standing on either side of a huge wicker garden chair. In the painting for which this pastel is a study (collection of Mr. David Daniels), Julie, the central figure in the composition, stands leaning over the garden fence. The wicker chair is turned sideways, and a watering can is casually added (see Pl. 13).

PLATE 14

JEANNE PONTILLON [1893]

Pastel, 13¾ x 16¾ in. (35 x 43 cm.)

Bibliography: Bataille no. 597.

Exhibited: p. Durand-Ruel 1896 no. 385; p. Dru 1926 no. 35.

One by one, the members of Berthe's family come under the scrutiny of her artistic eye as she measures their growth, physical and spiritual, and probes their characters in a series of revealing portraits. Jeanne Pontillon was her sister Edma's daughter and in the various portraits for which she sat to her aunt, Jeanne's resemblance to her cousin Julie is striking. The brilliant highlights of orange contrasting with her black hair severely pulled back give this portrait great energy and intensity, but the faraway look suggests a thoughtful, introspective mind. This pastel is one of several studies for the oil painting (B. 338).

PLATE 43

STUDY FOR "GIRL AMONG THE TULIPS"

Pastel, 16⅝ x 11⅞ in. (42 x 30 cm.) ; atelier stamp lower left.

Gabrielle Dufour, whom Berthe Morisot first saw carrying a bowl of milk. was equally at home in the meadow with her goats, in the garden playing with Julie, or seated in a field of tulips. Here with her "air sauvage" she has an almost oriental look, as, with eyes slanting, she squints into the sunlight. The pastel is a study for a painting in the collection of A. Conger Goodyear.

PLATE 46

HEAD OF A CHILD [1882]

Pastel, 18½ x 13½ in. (47 x 34 cm.) ; atelier stamps lower left (Lugt 1826 and 388a).

Bibliography: Bataille 468.

One recalls that Morisot, as one of the "mad" group of Impressionists had scandalized Paris in the 1870's. The shocked art critic for *Figaro* wrote: "Five or six lunatics, one of whom is a woman . . .", ending his piece with: "There is also a woman in the group, as is the case with all famous gangs. Her name is Berthe Morisot, and she is interesting to behold. In her, feminine grace is preserved amidst the frenzy of a mind in delirium."

Here the artist has with "frenzy" caught the play of light on the child's face and hair, imparting a feeling of extraordinary mobility to the features. The inverted page shows a first outline attempt, apparently begun too high on the page.

Berthe Morisot
B.M.

Berthe Morisot

The Drawings of Berthe Morisot

by DENIS ROUART

Anyone interested in the graphic work of Berthe Morisot is bound to notice at once the wealth of this material dating from the last five years of her life, in contrast to the almost total absence of drawings dating from her earlier career. The obvious explanation that first comes to mind is that her later works had a better chance to survive than her youthful attempts, but a careful analysis of her style leads to a different conclusion. That an artist should be negligent in preserving what might be considered immature jottings or even early sketches, is easily understood; but that she should have destroyed, systematically, all the preliminary studies done for paintings executed when she was at the height of her mature power—ten marvellously productive years—defies explanation. And then again why should she have so carefully preserved—one is tempted to say, hoarded—every drawing, pastel and water-color done between the years 1889 and 1895?

The careful student of her work is forced to accept a conclusion that is as logical as it is inevitable: the fact that she almost completely disregarded draftsmanship as a medium of expression prior to the year 1889. For if one takes into account the fact that this date also marks precisely the sharp break in the evolution of her *oeuvre* one is no longer groping for an answer to this most puzzling situation.

Launched on her career by the impetus of Corot's approval, and subject to his influence, then orienting herself along the lines of Manet's principles, Berthe Morisot became, in the period between 1878 to 1879, an artistic personality in her own right, striking out new paths for herself which she steadily followed from then on.

Her impressionist vision led her to adopt an idiom that was free and nervous, characterized by bold brush strokes, as though the brush, jabbing at the canvas, left dabs of pigment behind, irregular, disjointed, corresponding only to the play of colored light as it struck her dazzled eyesight. If this painterly idiom differs radically from the smaller, more orderly brush strokes of the Impressionist technique, it nevertheless stems from the same conception and has the same purpose: to render the sensation of color in the most direct and faithful manner possible.

We can therefore assume with logic and almost certainty that it was this avowed purpose which prompted Berthe Morisot to attack her canvas on the spot—without first preparing studies, sketching rough drafts, or making careful working drawings. Applying directly the touches of pigment which correspond to the colors that struck her retina, she found, by synthesizing these dabs of color, the structure and form of the objects portrayed, painting only that which her eyes actually perceived rather than that which her senses had preconceived. There were times, of course, when she drew on her canvas, with careful brush strokes, the precise outline for a painted composition. But this would serve only as a frame of reference, helping her delimit the bounds of her subject matter, preventing her from straying too far into one dimension or another while reconstructing this universe apprehensible only through so many flecks of color.

The stylistic idiom created by a bold and nervous brush which marks all her painted compositions between 1878 and 1888, seeming actually to correspond more to her own personal temperament than to the Impressionist vision, makes it difficult to foresee the radical change which her work was to undergo by 1888-1889. The transition from short, rapid brush strokes to long, sinuous ones is more than just a superficial change in technique; it speaks, rather, of a profoundly altered outlook and aim. It is, in fact, a clear statement of her new preoccupation with line and form.

From now on the supple arabesque defines the form, whereas before the brush strokes merely touched upon it. This drastic transformation of purpose makes both the absence of drawings from her early period and their abundance later on not only comprehensible, but perfectly logical, corresponding as it does to Berthe Morisot's development as a painter. Aside from a certain number of pencil sketches, her drawings, done mostly in black or red chalk (fusain or sanguine) are preliminary studies for paintings, and like those react against the flickering broken palette of Impressionism.

Pure in line, strong and solid, these drawings of young women and children in the fields, gardens or interiors of their homes, are a hymn to grace, as is all of Berthe Morisot's work.

PLATE VII

Collection of Sterling and Francine Clark Art Institute, Williamstown, Mass.

PLATE VIII

Berthe Morisot

CHRONOLOGY

1841	Born January 14th in Bourges.
	Lives in Limoges from 1841 until 1848.
1848	Lives in Paris.
1849	Lives in Caen.
1851	Lives in Rennes.
1852	Begins permanent residence in Paris about this time.
1857	Begins formal study of art with Chocarne.
	Leaves Chocarne to study with Guichard. Copies wash drawings of Gavarni after reproductions found in father's library. Visits Louvre with Guichard.
1858	In spring begins copying at Louvre under Guichard's instruction. Meets Bracquemond and Fantin-Latour at Louvre. Admires paintings by Rousseau, Daubigny, Millet, and especially Corot.
1860	Eager to paint out-of-doors, begins study with Corot.
1861	Spends summer with family at Ville d'Avray in order to be near Corot. Is lent paintings by Corot which she copies.
	Corot becomes frequent guest at Morisot family home on Rue Franklin, dining there every Tuesday.
1862	Spends summer in Pyrenees with sister Edma, where she travels about on mule and horseback and paints landscape.
	Continues lessons with Corot.
1863	Spends summer at Le Chou between Pontoise and Auvers. Is instructed there by Oudinot, a disciple of Corot. Corot cannot be there because of trip he is planning. During summer meets Daubigny and Daumier. Destroys most work from this period.
	During winter, for a period of about six months, studies sculpture with Aimé Millet. Models for architectural medallion which Millet is making.

1864 Father appointed chief councillor of Cour des Comptes. Family moves to other side of Rue Franklin. Father has studio for her built in garden. Exhibits in Paris Salon for first time; shows two landscapes.
Spends summer at Beauzeval in Normandy where father rents windmill. Landlord is painter Leon Riesener.
Mme. Morisot's Tuesday dinners attended by Charles and Jules Ferry, the Alfred Stevenses, and Carolus Duran. Rossini also a guest.
Attends receptions given by Rossini who appreciates her musical talent.

1865 Exhibits again at Paris Salon; shows two paintings. Is listed in catalog as student of Guichard and Oudinot.
Visits Chartres. Stays at the Petites Dalles in Fécamp and at Beauzeval.

1866 Exhibits two paintings at Paris Salon.
Visits Brittany. Paints at Rosbras and Douarnenez.

1867 Exhibits at Paris Salon where Manet is impressed with her "View of Paris from the Trocadero."
Eldest sister Yves marries.
Again visits Brittany.

PLATE IX

1868 Exhibits one painting at Paris Salon.
Continues to instruct herself at Louvre where she copies Rubens' "Exchange of the Two Princesses".
Is formally introduced to Edouard Manet by Fantin-Latour.
Manet and Morisot families become close friends. Morisots attend Mme. Auguste Manet's Thursday receptions where they meet Baudelaire, Degas, Charles Cros, Zola, Astruc, Bosc, Emanuel Chabrier, as well as the Alfred Stevenses, the Edouard Manets and Edouard's brothers, Gustave and Eugène.
Is introduced to Puvis de Chavannes by Stevens.
Becomes constant fellow worker of Edouard Manet. They mutually influence each other: she begins increasing emphasis on representation of modern life and freer handling of brush, he begins to work more out-of-doors and use more polychromatic palette.
Poses for Manet's "The Balcony" (now in Louvre).

1869 Sends nothing to Paris Salon.
Manet's "The Balcony" exhibited in Paris Salon.
Degas makes portrait of Yves Morisot.
Edma Morisot marries Adolphe Pontillon.
Spends summer at Lorient with Edma. Makes short trip to environs of Brest.
Offers Manet painting done in Lorient.

1870 Exhibits two paintings in Paris Salon.
Remains in Paris with family during War of 1870. Health permanently impaired by privations of period.
Takes up water-color painting. Copies fan given to her by Degas.

1871 Goes to Saint-Germain with family during Commune.
In May visits sister Edma at Cherbourg.
Again works at studio of sculptor Aimé Millet.
Exhibits in Paris Salon.

1872 Spends summer in Basque country at Saint-Jean-de-Luz with sister Yves. Finds country there pictorially monotonous.
Visits Spain. Goes to Madrid, Toledo, and the Escorial. Is impressed by works of Goya and Velasquez.
Visits sister Edma at Maurecourt.
Family moves to Rue Guichard about this time.

1873 Exhibits one pastel at Paris Salon.
Spends part of summer at Maurecourt with Edma.

1874 Father dies on January 24th.
Against Manet's protest, participates in organization of first impressionist group exhibition along with Monet, Pissarro, Sisley, Renoir, Degas, Cezanne, and Guillaumin. Although it had always accepted her work, agrees never to exhibit in Paris Salon again. Exhibits nine works in exhibition which opens on April 15th and is held at Nadar's, 35 Boulevard des Capucines.
Divides summer between Maurecourt and Fécamp where she and her mother visit the Manet family. Becomes engaged to Eugène Manet, younger brother of Edouard.
In autumn her portrait is painted several times by Edouard Manet.
Degas paints Eugène Manet and gives painting to Eugène and Berthe when they marry in December.

1875 Holds one-day auction sale of works at Hôtel Drouot on March 24th, together with Monet, Renoir, and Sisley. Sends twelve canvases. Her works gain highest prices of sale, but sale is failure in general.
In spring visits Gennevilliers, where Manet family owns land; and England where she stays at Ramsgate and the Isle of Wight. In London visits National Gallery where she is impressed with paintings by Turner, Wilkie, Gainsborough, and Hogarth. Also admires Whistler.
She and husband occupy Mme. Morisot's apartment at No. 7 Rue Guichard.

1876 Exhibits twenty works at second impressionist group exhibition held in April at No. 11, rue Le Peletier. Wolf writes article in the *Figaro* referring to Berthe and the impressionists as "five or six lunatics, one of whom is a woman."
Edouard Manet is rejected by Paris Salon.
About this time spends summers in Maurecourt, near Paris.
Her mother dies in October.
Moves closer to center of Paris where she and husband rent apartment at No. 9, Avenue d'Eylau (now Avenue Victor Hugo).

1877 Exhibits twenty works at third impressionist group exhibition, held in April at No. 6, Rue Le Peletier.

1878 Birth of her only child, Julie Manet, on November 14th.

1879 Weakened health caused by birth of her child, prevents her from preparing for fourth impressionist group exhibition. Is only time she does not participate.
Spends summer at Beauzeval-Houlgate.

1880 Exhibits fifteen works at fifth impressionist group exhibition, held in April at No. 10, Rue des Pyramides.
Again spends summer at Beauzeval-Houlgate.

1881 Exhibits several oils and several pastels at sixth impressionist group exhibition, held in April at No. 35, Boulevard des Capucines.
Spends summer at Bougival in rented house at No. 4, Rue de la Princesse.
Buys lot on Rue de Villejust and begins to build house.
Spends winter of 1881-1882 at Nice in Hotel Richmond.

1882 Works at Nice during winter.
At beginning of spring travels to Italy where she visits Genoa and Pisa. Is forced to suspend trip in Florence because of daughter's illness and cannot visit Venice.
Returns to Nice until middle of March for daughter's period of recuperation. Husband goes to Paris and prepares her entries for seventh impressionist group exhibition held during March at 251 Rue St.-Honoré, at which she exhibits nine paintings and pastels.
Rents small furnished apartment at No. 3, Rue du Mont-Thabor near Tuileries and remains there until going to Bougival for summer and winter of 1882-83 while awaiting completion of new house.

1883 Edouard Manet dies on April 30.
Moves into new house at 40 Rue de Villejust. Her visitors there include Renoir, Mallarmé, Degas, Monet, Caillebotte, Theodore Duret, Puvis de Chavannes, and Whistler.
About this time Monet promises her a painting for her new house.
Spends summer at Bougival.
In the fall three of her works included in impressionist exhibition in London.
Devotes winter of 1883-84 to organizing exhibition and, later, sale of works by Edouard Manet.

1884 Exhibition of Edouard Manet's works opens at the Ecole des Beaux-Arts on January 5th.
Buys several of Edouard Manet's paintings at unsuccessful auction of works from his studio which is held at Hôtel Drouot.
Spends last summer at Bougival.

1885 Visits sister Yves at Vieux Moulin in Forest of Compiègnes.
Goes to Belgium and Holland; is especially impressed by paintings of Rubens, Boucher, Perronneau, Reynolds, and Romney. Is disappointed in works by Hals.
Frequently entertains Degas, Monet, Renoir, and Mallarmé at her home in Paris. Also friendly with Mary Cassatt and the Emile Olliviers.

PLATE X

1886 In January visits Renoir's studio where she is impressed by the number and beauty of his drawings. Begins to put increasing emphasis on drawing.
She and husband take active part in organization of eighth and last impressionist group exhibition, held during May and June at No. 1, Rue Lafitte. Exhibits several paintings and a series of watercolors.
Spends June on Isle of Jersey.
Her works shown by Durand-Ruel in New York.
Again paints at Louvre where she copies Boucher's "Vulcan Presenting Venus with Arms Forged for Aeneas".
Continues to entertain her artist friends and Mallarmé at Thursday dinners.
Exhibits in New York during spring in Durand-Ruel's "Works in Oil and Pastel by the Impressionists of Paris".
Later shows in George's Petit's "Exposition Internationale" in Paris which also includes works by Whistler, Cazin, and Rodin. Exhibits paintings and one of her few sculptures.

1887 Renoir does portrait of her daughter holding cat.
Exhibits in Petit's "Exposition Internationale" with Sisley, Renoir, Monet, Pissarro, Whistler, Raffaëlli and others.
During summer visits Mallarmé at his farmhouse at Les Plâtreries.

In August visits Touraine and principal châteaux along. Loire Also visits Sarthe.

Continues as hostess of Thursday dinners. The Emile Olliviers join regular guests. Occasional guests are Astruc, Fantin-Latour, and Puvis de Chavannes.

Mallarmé asks her, Degas, Renoir, Monet, and Lewis-Brown to illustrate edition of his prose poems. Project is never carried out.

1888 Suffers severe illness toward end of winter of 1887-1888.

Exhibits three paintings, a pastel, and a watercolor at Durand-Ruel's exhibition in spring.

Remains in Paris throughout summer.

Desire to paint exotic vegetation attracts her to south of France. Rents villa on Riviera at Cimiez where she spends winter of 1888-1889. Series of eight drypoint etchings dates from this period.

1889 Returns to Paris from Riviera in the spring.

During spring and summer often visits Exposition Universelle. Is particularly impressed with Javanese dancers and the retrospective exhibition which includes gallery of work by Edouard Manet.

Interrupts summer only with visit to Sarthe.

Co-operates with Monet in attempt to have one of Manet's paintings bought by state.

About this time alters technique toward emphasis on drawing of form as well as rendering of light.

About this time Monet and Caillebotte, Mallarmé, Renoir, Degas, and Desboutin continue as regular guests at her home.

1890 Because of husband's poor health, rents house outside of Paris, at Mézy, in the spring. Remains there until autumn. Renoir visits her several times at Mézy and often shares same model. Mallarmé also stays with them.

Visits Monet at Giverny with her husband and Mallarmé.

Works all summer with view to publishing series of drawings of daughter.

Attempts to make color prints. Is disappointed in result.

About this time begins to work frequently in colored crayon.

Regnier and Wyzewa join her regular Thursday dinner guests.

At end of year is very ill.

1891 In early spring returns to Mézy. Again visited there by Renoir who also makes studies after nature.

1892 Buys 17th-century château at Mesnil à Juziers, between Meulon and Mantes.

Husband dies on April 13th.

Goes to château at Mesnil where she remains for a month.

Her first one-man exhibition held at Joyant's (Boussod and Valadon) from May 25th until June 18th. Leaves Paris day after opening, which she does not attend. Exhibition includes 43 works hung in two small galleries. Several works lent by collectors. Numerous works sold.

Monet buys "The Bowl of Milk."
Returns to Paris for summer.
In autumn takes daughter on trip to Touraine. Copies Boucher and Mantegna in museum at Tours. Admires paintings by Rubens, Delacroix.
On return to Paris, moves to No. 10, Rue Weber.

1893 In June eldest sister Yves dies.
In late August and in September visits Mallarmé at Valvins near Forest of Fontainbleau.
Visits Sisley at Moret with Mallarmé.
Spends day with Monet at Giverny in October. Sees his series of twenty-six cathedrals.
Continues to entertain her regular guests in new apartment.
Occasionally dines at Degas' where she usually meets Forain and Bartholomé.
Of newer generation of artists especially admires work of Maurice Denis.

1894 Receives first official recognition: her painting "Young Woman in Ball Dress" (1880) which had been shown in fifth impressionist exhibition, is purchased from Duret collection for Luxembourg Museum. Mallarmé is instrumental in its purchase.
In March visits Brussels where several of her paintings are being exhibited.
In August rents house not far from fishing port of Portrieux in Brittany.
In October buys portrait of herself by Manet on occasion of Duret collection auction.
Renoir paints portrait of her with daughter, and gives it to her as present.

1895 Dies on March 2nd after catching illness from daughter which becomes complicated with pneumonia. Names Renoir guardian of Julie.
According to Berthe's wishes, Julie returns to family home on Rue de Villejust where she lives with cousins.

NOTE TO CATALOG ENTRIES

In statements of dimension, sight measure is described, and height precedes width.
Angoulvent: refers to the published catalog of Berthe Morisot's work; Bataille: refers to the forthcoming catalog by Bataille and Wildenstein.
Because of the cursory nature of some exhibition catalog entries, difficulty in establishing exact exhibition records has often been encountered. When, for this reason, absolute identification of works is impossible but descriptive data conform sufficiently to suggest possible identity, the entry here is preceded by the letter: p. More specific data should be available in the forthcoming volume by Bataille and Wildenstein which will have the added benefit of Mme. Ernest Rouart's assistance.
Atelier stamp refers to the mark placed by the artist's family on works found unsigned after her death.

PLATE XI

Berthe Morisot

SELECTION OF BERTHE MORISOT'S MAJOR EXHIBITIONS

1864	Paris Salon: Exhibited two paintings.
1865	Paris Salon: Two paintings.
1866	Paris Salon: Two paintings.
1867	Paris Salon: One painting.
1868	Paris Salon: One painting.
1870	Paris Salon: Two paintings.
1872	Paris Salon: One pastel.
1873	Paris Salon: One pastel.
1874	First impressionist group exhibition, 35, boulevard des Capucines. Nine works, including two pastels and three watercolors.
1875	Paris: Auction sale, with Monet, Sisley, and Renoir; Hôtel Drouot. Twelve works.
1876	Paris: Second impressionist group exhibition, 11, rue Le Peletier. Nineteen works, including three watercolors and three pastels.
1877	Paris: Third impressionist group exhibition, 6, rue le Peletier. Nineteen works, including at least ten pastels, three watercolors, and two drawings.
1880	Paris: Fifth impressionist group exhibition, 10, rue des Pyramides. Fifteen paintings and watercolors.
1881	Paris: Sixth impressionist group exhibition, 35, boulevard des Capucines. Seven pastels and paintings.
1882	Paris: Seventh impressionist group exhibition, 251, rue Saint-Honoré. Nine paintings and pastels.
1883	London: Dowdeswell and Dowdeswell (organized by Durand-Ruel). Group exhibition. Three works by Berthe Morisot.
1886	Paris: Eighth impressionist group exhibition, 1, rue Laffitte. Eleven paintings, series of watercolors, drawings, and fans.

Paris: George Petit. Exposition internationale. Group exhibition.

New York: Durand-Ruel. "Works in Oil and Pastel by the Impressionists of Paris." Catalog lists 310 works, including nine by Berthe Morisot.

1887 Paris: George Petit. Exhibition internationale.

1892 Paris: Boussod and Valadon (Joyant). First one-man exhibition. Forty-three works.

1896 Paris: Durand-Ruel. First posthumous one-man exhibition. At least 191 paintings, 61 pastels, 64 drawings, 73 watercolors, two sculptures, three copies of works by other masters.

1900 Paris: Exposition internationale universelle. Represented in impressionists' gallery.

1902 Paris: Durand-Ruel. One-man exhibition. Fifty-eight paintings, seven pastels, thirteen watercolors.

1905 London: Grafton (organized by Durand-Ruel). Group show. 278 works by nine artists including Berthe Morisot.

1914 Copenhagen: Royal Museum. "Exposition d'art français du XIXe siècle." 356 works including five by Berthe Morisot.

1917 Zurich: Kunsthaus. "Franzosische Kunst des XIX und XX Jahrhunderts." 362 works, including five by Berthe Morisot.

1922 Paris: Marcel Bernheim. One-man exhibition. Fifty-seven paintings, eighteen watercolors, twelve pastels and drawings, eight drypoints, portrait of Berthe Morisot by Manet.

1924 Pittsburgh: Carnegie Institute. "Exhibition of Paintings by Edouard Manet/Pierre Renoir/Berthe Morisot." Forty-two paintings, including twenty by Berthe Morisot.

1926 Paris: L. Dru. One-man exhibition. Thirty-eight pastels, 40 watercolors, 20 drawings, thirteen colored-crayon drawings.

1929 Paris: Bernhein-Jeune. One-man exhibition. 101 paintings, 39 watercolors, 24 pastels, 22 drawings, eight drawings in colored-crayon, one sculpture.

1930 Amsterdam: Stedelijk Museum. "Vincent Van Gogh en zijn tijd genooten." 314 works, including nine by Berthe Morisot.

London: Leicester Galleries. One-man exhibition. Twenty-two paintings; 32 watercolors, drawings, pastels, drypoints; etching of Berthe Morisot by Edouard Manet.

New York: Durand-Ruel. "Paintings by Mary Cassatt and Berthe Morisot." Twenty-two paintings, including eleven by Berthe Morisot.

1932 London: Royal Academy of Arts. "French Art, 1200-1900." 1027 works, including six paintings, one watercolor, one pastel by Berthe Morisot.

1934 New York: Durand-Ruel. "Exhibition of Paintings by the Master Impressionists." Thirty-one paintings, including three by Berthe Morisot.

1936 New York: Wildenstein. One-man exhibition. Twenty-four paintings, eleven watercolors, five drawings.

London: Knoedler. One-man exhibition. Forty-three paintings, nine pastels, twenty-two watercolors, sixteen drawings.

1937 New York: Carroll Carstairs. One-man exhibition. Paintings, drawings, pastels, watercolors.

1938 Boston: Goodman-Walker. One-man exhibition. Watercolors and drawings.

1939 New York: Durand-Ruel. "Exhibition of Paintings of Berthe Morisot and Mary Cassatt." Six works by Berthe Morisot.

1941 Paris: Musée de l'Orangerie. One-man exhibition. 122 paintings, 38 pastels, 59 watercolors, 19 drawings in colored-crayon, 45 drawings in other media, nine prints, one sculpture.

1943 Chicago: The Arts Club of Chicago. One-man exhibition. Nineteen oil paintings, three watercolors, five drawings, one pastel, two etchings.

1946 Paris: Quatre Chemins. One-man exhibition. Watercolors.

1948 Paris: Durand-Ruel. One-man exhibition. Eighty-one pastels, watercolors, and drawings.

1949 Copenhagen. Ny-Carlsberg Glyptotek. One-man exhibition. Fifty-one paintings, thirty-three drawings, pastels, and watercolors, portrait of Berthe Morisot by Edouard Manet.

Stockholm: National Museum. One-man exhibition. Same as Copenhagen, plus one *tilfojelse.*

1950 London: The Arts Council of Great Britain. One-man exhibition. Fifty-three paintings, twenty-three drawings, watercolors, and pastels.

1951 Geneva: Motte. One-man exhibition. At least twenty-two works, including paintings, watercolors, and drawings.

1952 Limoges: Musée municipal. "Homage à Berthe Morisot et Pierre-August Renoir." Thirty-seven works by Berthe Morisot, including three drawings and pastels.

1952—ff., Toronto, Montreal, New York, Toledo, Washington, San Francisco, Portland, Los Angeles, Minneapolis, Kansas City, Winnipeg, Buffalo, The Art Gallery of Toronto, Montreal Museum of Fine Arts, The Metropolitan Museum of Art, The Toledo Museum of Art, The Phillips Collection, California Palace of the Legion of Honor, Portland Art Museum, Los Angeles County Museum, Minneapolis Institute of Arts, William Rockhill Nelson Gallery, Winnipeg Art Gallery, Albright Art Gallery. "Berthe Morisot and her circle/Paintings from the Rouart Collection, Paris." Twenty paintings by Berthe Morisot, seven paintings by Edouard Manet, one painting each by Edgar Degas, Claude Monet, and Auguste Renoir.

1957 Dieppe: Musée de Dieppe. One-man exhibition. Sixty paintings, thirteen watercolors, two pastels, nine drawings, one drypoint, letters and photographs.

1958 Albi: Musée Toulouse-Lautrec. One-man exhibition. Sixty-three paintings, twenty-seven pastels and watercolors, thirteen drawings, sketch books, letters from Degas, Renois, Manet quatrain by Mallarmé.

PLATE XII

GENERAL WORKS

Duret, Theodore: *Manet and the French Impressionists,* Philadelphia, 1910; xi, 279, (1) pp., frontispiece, 38 pl. Includes brief chapter on Berthe Morisot.
Rewald, John: *The History of Impressionism,* New York, 1946; 474 pp. profusely illustrated, some color plates. Includes chronologies of impressionists in relation to world events, as well as general and monographic bibliographies.
Valéry, Paul: *Degas/Manet/Morisot,* New York, 1960 (vol. 12 of Bollingen Series XLV "The Collected Works of Paul Valéry") ; xxxiv, 261 pp., not illus. Translated by David Paul. Includes two essays on Berthe Morisot, "Tante Berthe" and "Berthe Morisot".
Wyzewa, Teodore de: *Peintres de jadis et d' aujourd'hui,* Paris, 1903; 387 pp. plus 18 pls. Includes brief essay on Berthe Morisot (pp. 213-220).

MONOGRAPHS

Angoulvent, Monique: *Berthe Morisot,* Paris, 1933; 164 pp., 15 pls. Includes preface by Robert Rey, extensive essay on life and work of Berthe Morisot, definitive catalog of 665 works, and texts of Berthe Morisot's certificates of birth, marriage, and death; extensive bibliography.
Bataille, M. L. and Wildenstein, G: *Catalogue complet de l'oeuvre de Berthe Morisot,* Paris, 1960 (forthcoming) ; 1 vol. containing 850 reprods. Prepared with the collaboration of the artist's daughter, Mme Ernest Rouart.
Forreau, Armand: *Berthe Morisot,* Paris, 1925 (one of the series "Maîtres de l'art moderne") ; 64 pp. plus 40 pls. Essay on life and work of Berthe Morisot. English translation by H. Wellington was published as *Berthe Morisot* (one of the series "Masters of Modern Art"), New York, 1925.
Rouart, Denis: *Correspondence de Berthe Morisot avec sa famille et ses amis Manet, Puvis de Chavannes, Degas, Monet, Renoir et Mallarmé,* Paris, 1950; 184 pp., plus 28 pls. (some in color) of drawings, watercolors, and prints by Morisot, Manet, Degas, and Renoir, plus facsimiles of letters, plus numerous drawings by Berthe Morisot within text. Text by Denis Rouart, grandson of Berthe Morisot and curator of the Musée des Beaux-Arts, Nancy, incorporates quotations of letters into discussion of life and work of Berthe Morisot. English translation by Betty W. Hubbard was published as *"The Correspondence of Berthe Morisot . . ."*, Wittenborn, New York, 1957.
Rouart, Denis: *Berthe Morisot,* Paris, (1948) (one of the series "Les maîtres") ; (12) pp. illustrated, plus 48 pls. Brief essay on life and work of Berthe Morisot is printed in French, English, and German.
Rouart, Louis: *Berthe Morisot,* Paris, 1941, (one of the series "Editions d'Histoire et d'Art"; 47 pp. including reproductions. Essay on the life and work of Berthe Morisot written by her nephew.
Seize Aquarelles, Paris, (1946) ; 16 pp. plus 16 color pls. Essays on Morisot by Mallarmé (untitled essay published originally in Durand-Ruel 1896 catalog *(q.v.)*) and Valéry (untitled essay published elsewhere as "Au sujet de Berthe Morisot" and as "Berthe Morisot").

EXHIBITION CATALOGS

Albi, Musée de Toulouse-Lautrec, 1958: *Exposition Berthe Morisot;* 106 pp. including 24 pls. and a photograph of Berthe Morisot in 1874. Introduction by Edouard Julien which comments on the relationship of Toulouse-Lautrec to Morisot; essay by Raymond Escholier "Berthe Morisot et sa magie".
Copenhagen, N. Y.-Carlsberg Glyptotek, 1949; *Berthe Morisot;* 25 pp. plus 6 pls. incl. photograph of Berthe Morisot in 1875. Foreword by Haavard Rostrup.
Dieppe, Musée de Dieppe, 1957: *Exposition Berthe Morisot;* ix., 10 pp. plus 6 pls. plus cover reproduction. Preface by Paul Valéry "Au sujet de Berthe Morisot".
Limoges, Musée Municipal, 1952; *Homage à Berthe Morisot et à Pierre-Auguste Renoir/* 47 pp. and XXXV pls. plus cover reproduction. Introduction by Serge Gauthier; essay by Denis Rouart "Renoir et Berthe Morisot" which describes personal and artistic relationships between Renoir and Morisot and quotes from their letters.
London, The Arts Council of Great Britain, 1950: *Berthe Morisot;* 19 pp. plus VIII pls. Introduction by Denis Rouart; unsigned chronology.
London, M. Knoedler & Co., Inc., 1936: *Berthe Morisot (Mme Eugène Manet);* (18) pp. incl. 6 reproductions. Unsigned preface.
London, The Leicester Galleries, 1930: *Catalog of the Berthe Morisot Exhibition;* 24 pp. plus 4 pls. Preface by Stéphane Mallarmé originally published in Durand-Ruel 1896 catalog *(q.v.),* brief unsigned biographical note.
Paris, Galerie L. Dru, 1926: *Exposition de Pastels—Aquarelles—Dessins—Crayons de Berthe Morisot;* 15 pp., no illus. Essay "Tante Berthe" by Paul Valéry.
Paris, Boussod et Valadon, 1892: *Exposition Berthe Morisot.* Preface by Gustave Geffroy.
Paris, Durand-Ruel, 1896: Berthe Morisot (Madame Eugène Manet) ; not paged, not illus. Preface by Stéphane Mallarmé.
Paris, Musée de l'Orangerie, 1941: *Berthe Morisot;* (53) pp. plus (9) pls. Preface by Paul Valéry "Au sujet de Berthe Morisot".
Stockholm, National Museum, 1949: *Berthe Morisot;* 27 pp. plus 6 pls. Foreword by Haavard Rostrup.
Toronto, The Art Gallery of Toronto, 1952: *Berthe Morisot and her circle/Paintings from the Rouart Collection, Paris;* (10) pp. 30 pls. Introduction by Denis Rouart (reprint of translation which appears in Arts Council catalog *(q.v.)*) ; "catalog notes prepared with assistance of Mme. Ernest Rouart, Denis Rouart, and John Rewald."

PLATE XIII Oil on canvas, 28¼ x 31¼. Collection of Mr. David Daniels.